Dedication

This book is dedicated to both the Creator of the Universe and my Family, who have been so inspiring, encouraging and incredibly patient with me through the unfolding of this story. I also want to thank all the characters who played their part with passion!

I AM SEQUOIA
A Pinecone's Adventure

*"I may be small in size,
but inside I feel incredibly large!"*

Written & Illustrated by
E.P. Clanton

Thank you for buying an authorized addition of this book and for complying with copyright laws by not scanning or reproducing any part of it in any form without permission. You are supporting writers and illustrators for their hard work by doing this.

All rights reserved. No part of this publication may be reproduced or transmitted in any form by any means without written permission from the publisher except in the case of brief quotations embodied in critical articles and reviews.

For information contact:
I Am Sequoia at www.iamsequoia.com
Eagle's Quest Books at www.eaglesquestbooks.com

Written and Illustrated by E.P. Clanton
Illustrations created with Graphite pencils & Prismacolor pencils on 100lb. Futura Cover Stock Matte

ISBN Hardcover: #978-0-578-81092-8
ISBN Softcover: #978-0-578-81093-5

Published by Eagle's Quest Books
Copyright © 2020 by E. P. Clanton

Copyright United States Copyright Office
Library of Congress Cataloging-in-Publication Data Available.
Case #: 1-9517040005
Title: I Am Sequoia, A Pinecone's Adventure

First Edition–2020

Printed in United States of America

10 9 8 7 6 5 4 3 2 1

Acknowledgments:

Josiah Clanton
Working Ostrich creative agency of Portland, Oregon
www.workingostrich.com

Nathanael Clanton
Clanton Brand of Vancouver, Washington
www.nathanaelclanton.com / www.frontrunners.life

Declaration:
No pinecones, trees, plants, seeds, animals or bugs were harmed in the development and creation of this story.

I am safe high above.

I see incredible sunrises and feel the warmth of the sun.

I also see the sky that looks like it's on fire with the most beautiful sunsets.

I am very high up!

I am joyful and comfortable.

I can see all the mountains,
it feels like I can touch the stars.

I am special,
I can see more than anyone.

I am strong!

Nothing can bring me down!

I begin hearing loud noises and then I see flashes of light cracking through the sky.

I am scared and feel unsafe.

Everything is getting cold and wet, the clouds are getting darker.
The sun is disappearing quickly.

I am closing up, I feel afraid and exposed.

The wind begins blowing wildly!
Everything is being shaken!

I am losing control and
my strength is fading.

Something snaps!

Suddenly... I am falling and
nothing is familiar anymore.

I close up really tight, I'm very
scared! I don't understand!

Before I know it,
I hit the ground so hard!

Crash!... Crunch!... Ouch!

I am broken and bruised!

I lay here confused and hurt
from what just happened to me.

I am all alone.

I feel disconnected from life
as I knew it.

I hear crashing, crunching and breaking sounds.

Out of the deep forest a very large bear is coming toward me.

I don't know what to do, so I try to hide.

Suddenly I am covered by a huge shadow.

I hear grumbling and growling sounds.

The bear is stepping on me,
pushing me under the ground!
I feel powerless!

I don't like this place!
It's cold, lonely and dark!

Why is this happening to me?

I try to get out but nothing works
and now I am getting tired.

It's very quiet here.
I am falling asleep now...
Goodnight.

I am having the strangest dream.
I feel the ground shake and rumble around me.

I am changing shapes and sprouting roots everywhere. Darkness suddenly bursts into light! I feel the warmth of the sun.

Waking up, I understand that this is no dream!
I am welcomed by new friends of all sizes and colors.

I am surprised that I have new branches growing! Now I can reach for the sky!

Sometimes I feel awkward and uncomfortable, but I am learning patience with all the new changes in my life.

I am not alone or fearful any more.

I feel very loved and accepted just as I am.

I am very thankful.

I feel like I've been planted right where I am supposed to be.

Life is good!

I am looking up from where
I was born.

These trees are so big they seem
to disappear into the clouds.

They look very friendly and kind.

I feel comfortable around them,
I feel I am one of them!

I may be small in size but inside,
I feel incredibly large!

I am growing stronger and bigger as the seasons pass.

My old friends have gone but I welcome new friends as they travel by.

Cold winter snow, icy rain and strong winds try to break me and bring me down.

I reach deep into the ground to spread my roots.

I feel protected, secure and loved!

I hear a gentle voice saying to me,
"I've been waiting for you.
Come on up, the view is amazing!"

Looking up, I see a giant tree.
"Who are you?" I ask.

"I am Sequoia. We are your family.
Welcome home!"

I keep reaching higher and higher
with all my new branches, growing
taller each day!

I am thankful for this old bear
traveling by again.

Many seasons ago he changed
my life by stepping on me,
everything became dark and cold!

I remember being so fearful,
I didn't understand. I wasn't sure
I would see another day.

Sometimes changes can be scary!

It's strange how things seem
to work out.

I am grateful for today!

Seasons have come and gone, my life has new meaning and I'll never be the same.

Life is an amazing adventure!

I am very humbled now to be the biggest tree in my world.

I can see everything around me.

I am alive, I am loved...

The End.

Want to learn more about Sequoias and how they grow? Go to our website for more information and special offers!

www.iamsequoia.com

About the Author

E. P. Clanton lives in Portland, Oregon where he enjoys the beautiful Pacific Northwest outdoors. He has an entrepreneurial background as an artist, multi-media craftsman and author.

He loves cooking, hiking, camping, traveling and spending time with his family, including playing and reading stories with his grandchildren.

CPSIA information can be obtained
at www.ICGtesting.com
Printed in the USA
BVHW021429080421
604474BV00005B/75